650

W9-BRA-149

MARBLING
ON FABRIC

MARBLING
ON FABRIC

DANIEL AND PAULA COHEN

with Eden Gray

 INTERWEAVE PRESS

Design by Signorella Graphics
Illustrations by Ann Sabin
Photography by Joe Coca

 INTERWEAVE PRESS
306 North Washington Avenue • Loveland, Colorado 80537

Library of Congress Cataloging-in-Publication Data

Cohen, Daniel, 1954–
    Marbling on fabric / Daniel and Paula Cohen.
      p. cm.
    Includes bibliographical references.
    ISBN 0-934026-54-8 : $12.95
      1. Textile printing. 2. Marbling. I. Cohen, Paula, 1951–
II. Title.
TT852.C64   1990
746.6'2—dc20   89-78121
                                        CIP

To Benjamin and Rachel,
and to all future marblers

C O N T E N T S

Introduction   11
History   13
Preparations   15
  Overview   15
  Set Up Your Work Space   16
    How to Build a Marbling Frame   17
  Assemble Your Supplies   18
  Buy Some Fabric   19
  Collect Combs, Whisks, and Other Tools   20
  Prepare the Medium   21
  Heated Carrageenan   22
  Blender Carrageenan   23
  Prepare the Fabric   24
  Prepare the Paint   25

The Magic Part   27
  Apply the Paint   27
  Make the Pattern   27
  Lay the Fabric   28
  Lift, Rinse, and Dry the Fabric   28
  Skim the Medium   29
  Clean Up   29
  Care of Marbled Fabrics   30
  Color Mixing   31
  The Marbling Process   32

Patterns   34
  Stone   35
  Freestyle   37
  Combed   39

Cascade   41
Nonpareil   43
Feather   45
Zebra   47
Bouquet   49
Wings   51
Wave   53
Shadow Marbling   55

Projects   56
   Project Number 1: Throw Pillows   57
   Project Number 2: T-Shirt with a Circular Motif   61
   Project Number 3: Note Cards   65
   Project Number 4: Pieced Jacket   69
   Project Number 5: Canvas Tennis Shoes   73
   Project Number 6: Silk Kimono   77

Tips and Techniques   81
   Other Media   82

Teaching   85

Appendices   89
   Glossary   89
   Bibliography   90
   Sources and Suppliers   91
   Checklist of Equipment and Supplies   92
   Index   93

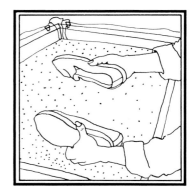

Antique Dutch Pattern

I N T R O D U C T I O N

I remember the first time I ever saw marbling. I was a child of five or six, looking at the endpapers of an old book. I had never seen anything so beautiful before. Every so often, as I grew up, I would see other marbled papers. I never stopped to think how they were made, but they always enchanted me.

A few years ago, my wife, Paula, and I visited my grandmother, Eden Gray, in Florida. She has been an artist, craftswoman, and teacher for many years, but she had recently discovered the world of textile arts. She had just taken a weekend workshop on marbling. Watching her work on sheets of paper or squares of silk, we were enthralled with the limitless variety and the beautiful flow of patterns achievable with this simple technique. Even as beginners, we got beautiful results. When we left we had marbled sheets, pillow cases, paper, and fabric swatches, and

only the greatest restraint spared our two small children from a colorful fate.

Paula and I returned home ready to begin this work ourselves, and thus started months of investigation and research. We did not get far. There was very little available information about marbling paper, and no books at all on marbling fabric. What we did find in print spoke of the hazards of dust, humidity, temperature, light—everything but the fullness of the moon. Some marbling supplies were not available in art supply stores. We ordered them from a mail-order house and mixed up several batches of gelatinous goo that never did quite what it was supposed to do. Not to be discouraged, Paula experimented with liquid starch, gelatin, egg whites, and several other common household substances, even diluted wallpaper paste. Then she tried different kinds of paints, fabric fixatives, and

water. But our results using these alternative substances were a far cry from the sharp, well-defined, bright patterns we had obtained in Florida.

Two years later Eden invited us back. More practiced at the art, she had taught the process to many others. Paula and I decided that perhaps, if we went through the entire marbling process together, making careful notes and testing our ideas on a variety of fabrics, we could write a book based on our findings and thus share the art with others.

Using the technique Eden showed us, we found that there are many variables in marbling, but it is not difficult to consistently get great results in any reasonably equipped workplace. We wrote this book to save you the frustration we endured.

Happy marbling. Enjoy!
Daniel Cohen

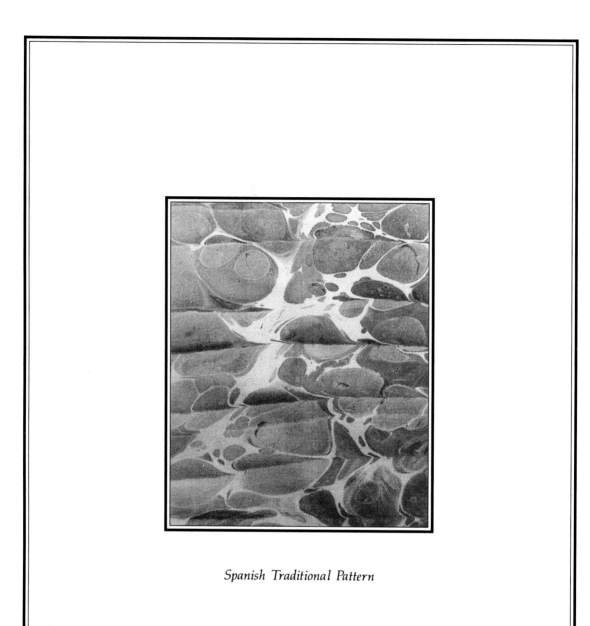

Spanish Traditional Pattern

The Japanese marbled paper 700 years ago using inks floating on water. The art is still being practiced there (look up "Suminagashi" in the *Encyclopaedia Britannica*; see *Suminagashi: An Introduction to Japanese Marbling* by Don Guyot). Some believe that the Chinese may have developed a marbling technique even earlier than the Japanese. There is also evidence that marbling was practiced in Persia several hundred years ago.

Sir Francis Bacon wrote in 1627 about papers the Turks were making with oil colors. At that time the English had very few colonies, and the Turks controlled half the world and most of its wealth. *Ebru*, as the Turks called the marbling process, was developed to protect their important documents from forgery. Like snowflakes and fingerprints, no two examples of marbling are ever exactly the same; when a calligrapher had finished inscribing a marbled sheet, even the smallest attempt to alter the document would have been easily detected. No wonder secrecy, ritual, and even religious or mystical significance have long been associated with marbling.

By the late 1700s, the Europeans had learned the art of marbling. Each country that took up the craft gave new twists and turns to the patterns, thus identifying the work with its country of origin. Pattern names such as Old Dutch, French Curl, and Spanish marbling are still recognized today. Marbled papers were used primarily as endpapers by bookbinderies and can still be found in fine older books.

A modern renaissance in bookbinding and decorative papers began in the 1960s, when marbled paper became popular in this country. In Spain, a cottage industry was launched to produce marbled papers that are exported for sale by the sheet for gift wrapping and note cards. Marbled papers are again being used as endpapers in fine books.

Now in the last decade of this century, we are seeing a renewed interest in fabric design. Like a flashback to the late 1960s, we see tie-dyed T-shirts, batiked blouses, and hand-decorated skirts and dresses. A few American designers are beginning to experiment with marbled silk, and are working small bits and strips of these fabrics into kimonos, dresses and quilts. Marbling kits are marketed in some craft stores.

When this new interest in home-crafted fabrics combines with the marbling directions on the following pages, perhaps we'll see a new fabric trend in the 1990s: the decade of marbled clothing.

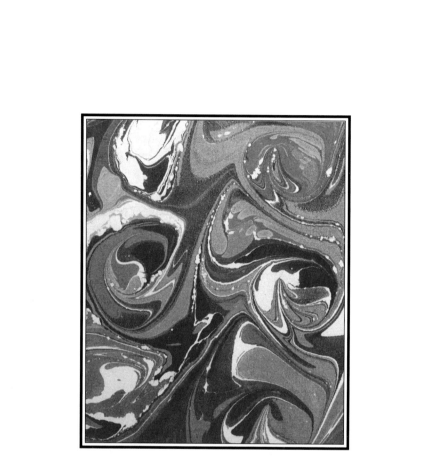

French Curl Pattern

The basic technique of marbling is simple.

The basic technique of marbling is simple. On a shallow vat of gelatinous medium (sometimes called a *size* or *marbling bath*), you float paints or inks of different colors. They form a surface film of colors that you then rake and swirl with combs, picks, or other simple tools to form a design. When the design is pleasing, you lay a pretreated piece of paper or cloth gently on the surface of the medium to pick up the paint. A simple rinse in clear water removes excess paint. Most paints or inks then need to be set, or made permanent, by resting and heating with an iron. The vat of medium is quickly skimmed with strips of newspaper and is ready for the next unique marbled print.

There are many variations on this basic procedure. There are different kinds of media, different kinds of ink and paint, and different methods of mingling the colors to form families of patterns. The materials we've found most effective, easy, and affordable include a medium made of carrageenan and water, cloth prepared with an alum solution, and acrylic paints diluted with water and mixed with a surfactant for the various color patterns.

These materials are nontoxic. Carrageenan, also called Irish moss, is a seaweed which thickens and stabilizes fluids. You'll find it in ice cream and yogurt. Some health food stores sell carrageenan. Alum (aluminum sulfate) is an astringent, used in making pickles. It's available in drugstores and grocery stores. Surfactants are wetting agents that break down the surface tension of a liquid. Our choice, oxgall, is used by water-colorists to thin their paint, and is available at art supply stores. Photo-flo, available at photography supply stores, is preferred by some fabric marblers.

Carrageenan may be hard to find locally, but it's readily available by mail order. This is often less expensive, and book-bindery or dye suppliers can usually offer more information or answer questions better than the local grocer or druggist. Mail-order sources of carrageenan, alum, and fabrics are listed on page 91.

We will describe our experiments with other materials such as wallpaper paste, egg whites, and liquid starch, and you'll see why we prefer carrageenan. After you gain some experience you may wish to try other methods yourself, but for your first several experiments we strongly urge you to stick to the tried-and-true materials and follow our instructions to the letter. Although marbling is simple, small variables do make a difference. Expect the unexpected, and don't give up if the first few pieces you do aren't exactly what you hoped they would be. Even "mistakes" in marbling can be quite lovely.

SET UP YOUR WORK SPACE

You'll need to gather some materials, equipment, and cloth before you can start marbling. We'll describe the set-up and marbling process here in the order you actually do the steps, but for your shopping convenience we've written a checklist on page 92 of the materials and equipment you will need.

Find a place that can be undisturbed for as long as your project will last. You may have some spills and splashes, so either use a room where you can drip or cover the floors below the table or counter with newspaper. Carrageenan medium is very slippery; avoid walking through the spots and spills.

A well-lit work area is important because you need to clearly see the paints being manipulated on the surface of the medium. Go for plenty of light without glare.

You will be using running water to rinse each piece that you take out of the medium, in addition to the water you use to set up and clean up. Having a sink in the room is ideal, but you could work in a garage with a garden hose nearby.

Set up your work space in a kitchen, workroom, garage, or yard.

In this work space you'll need a table or counter to hold your shallow vat of medium at a reasonable working height. The table or counter should be big enough to hold not only the vat but also several small bottles of paint, a collection of small tools for swirling the paint, and a stack of newspaper strips for skimming the medium between prints. If you will be doing large pieces of fabric, you will need space to walk around your project.

You'll need a clothesline, preferably outside where the drips won't matter, and a lightweight bowl or bucket to carry dripping wet marbled fabric to the sink and then to the clothesline. On a few fabrics, the freshly marbled surface is more delicate, and you may need to lay your pieces flat on a plastic-covered piece of cardboard to carry it to the sink and the clothesline. So have a drip bucket ready and make the waterproof cardboard tray later if you need it.

When we began to marble, several people cautioned us about the immediate climate of the work area. We had read that the ideal temperature is around 65°F (18°C), and that the humidity should be high to minimize the amount of dust in the air. While these factors merit consideration, we have marbled in the summer in dry, warm (78°F) air and have not noticed the climate to be a significant factor.

HOW TO BUILD A MARBLING FRAME

You will need a container to hold the carrageenan medium. You can easily begin experimenting with a simple kitchen dishpan, about 14 inches by 18 inches, and no more than 2 gallons of distilled water to make the first batch of medium. The container must be a light color so that you can see the paints on the surface as you work. Since the vat of medium must be big enough to lay the full piece you are marbling out flat, a dishpan will work only for small projects.

For marbling bigger pieces, it's easy to build a marbling frame, a rectangle of wood that holds a plastic liner. The dimensions of this marbling frame can vary according to the size and shape of the material you want to marble. We recommend a frame no larger than necessary to lay out your largest piece of fabric. You will be filling the frame with about 1 1/2 to 2 inches of medium, and the larger the frame, the more carrageenan and paints you will need to fill it. Thus, it is most economical to use the smallest reasonable size. It will also give you the most satisfactory results. Color placed on the medium thins and spreads until it reaches the sides of the frame; a small frame contains the paints and facilitates bright, detailed patterning. Fur-

It's easy to build a frame of any size you want for your marbled projects, using wood, iron corner angles, and clear plastic.

ther, the smaller the frame, the more the surface tension of the medium supports the paint, causing more of it to sit on the surface instead of sinking to the bottom.

So build your marbling frame slightly larger (say 1 inch on each side) than the largest piece of fabric you expect to color. For instance, if you plan to marble 36-inch-square silk scarves, make your frame 38 inches square.

We have used frames with attached bottoms, and open-bottomed frames designed to sit on tables. The former is sturdier, but heavier and more difficult to move about, and much harder to empty out.

We recommend using 1-inch by 4-inch framing wood (the kind found in all home improvement stores) for the sides, with a white or clear plastic lining and no attached bottom. Cut the wood to the lengths you need for the sides, and use flat metal angles screwed into the wood to make the square corners. Place this frame on a light surface on your table. Put the lining in the frame making neat folds at the corners, and hold the lining in place with a few push pins along the top edge of the wood. Make sure that there is enough liner to reach to the bottom of each inner side, but not so much that it is buckling up in the middle of the frame. At the corners, tuck and fold the plastic so that it conforms to the sides of the frames as closely as possible. The lining can be a clear or white 2-mil drop cloth, shower curtain lining, or sheet of plastic. Make sure that there are no sharp edges inside the frame; you don't want to puncture the plastic liner and end up with a room full of goo.

In classroom settings, we've seen small, medium and large frames constructed from lengths of inch-thick styrofoam glued or taped together and lined with plastic. Heavy cardboard boxes lined with plastic can also be used. Because these are inexpensive and easy to make and store, you could have several in different sizes for your various projects.

For long lengths of fabric, we've even heard of people using children's plastic inflatable swimming pools. No liner would be necessary, but bailing it out would take a while!

You'll need carrageenan, alum, distilled water, oxgall, and acrylic paints.

ASSEMBLE YOUR SUPPLIES

You'll need carrageenan, alum, distilled water, oxgall, and acrylic paints. We recommend that you buy the carrageenan and alum from a mail-order supplier (see Sources and Suppliers, page 91). A half pound of each will do several batches of fabrics. When ordering carrageenan, be sure to ask the distributor if it is blender carrageenan or if it needs to be cooked. Both will work well and we include instructions for each, but the methods are slightly different so you'll need to know which one you have.

Use distilled water the first several times. It will give you a predictable mix with the carrageenan regardless of your local water supply. After you begin to get consistently good results from your experiments, you can try your tap water to see if your results are still good or if local mineral or chemical impurities spoil your marbling. Distilled water is available in grocery stores; three gallons will be enough for your first marbling bath.

We use inexpensive water-based, nontoxic acrylic paints, found in craft stores everywhere. We have also used medium-range to expensive paints, and some claiming to be especially prepared for marbling. We have tried fabric dyes and airbrush paints. Some inexpensive acrylics don't interact well and can't be manipulated for long before drifting away into grainy puddles. So buy a small amount and test first. In general, if the label says that it can be used on fabric, it will probably work just fine for marbling (see Sources and Suppliers, page 91).

We have found that we can't use colors made by different paint or dye companies in the same bath. Because the weights vary, if we place airbrush dyes on the surface of the medium, drops of acrylic paint will fall right through to the bottom of the frame. Colors from one brand of paint will work only with other colors of that brand; when we've tried to add even one other color from another brand, the whole vat has gone grainy and patterns are impossible to manipulate past the simple swirl stage.

Airbrush dyes have some other peculiarities. They produce vivid, gorgeous, translucent colors and can be dripped straight out of the bottle without mixing of any kind. They are smelly, though, and so light in weight that they drift gradually throughout the medium like fine ribbons of color; after only a few applications, the vat is so murky that it's not possible to distinguish what is on the surface from what is on the bottom or drifting just below the surface. The edges of individual drops tend to feather and

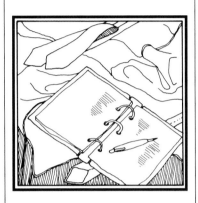

You can marble on fabric yardage, ready-made silk scarves or neckties, or any of the objects shown in the project section later in the book. It's easiest to start with flat fabric, though. Take notes as you do your first experimental pieces.

fan and not remain intact as clearly defined circles or bands of color, but they are readily manipulated into fine patterns.

Oxgall and acrylic paints are available from art supply stores. A small bottle of oxgall and a small container of each of several colors in a single brand of paint will last you through several projects.

BUY SOME FABRIC

In general, the more finely textured the fabric, the more precisely the cloth picks up the marbled pattern from the surface of the medium. Coarser materials pick up the patterns, but with less clearly defined edges. Napped or heavily textured fabrics such as velvets, corduroys, or nubbed cottons will yield unpredictable and probably disappointing results.

Natural or synthetic fibers both work. We like silk best, particularly for scarves, ties, and items to be sold at art fairs and boutiques, but synthetic satins also take the pattern from the medium very well, and the resulting fabric is highly suited for projects that require a medium- to heavyweight fabric. Prehemmed silk scarves and silk yardage are available by mail from some of the companies listed on page 91.

Pure linen and cotton work well too, but when we have printed T-shirts with acrylic paints, cotton/polyester knits have printed better than all-cotton ones. However, when we've used squeeze-bottle fabric dyes instead of acrylic paints, we've got equally good results on all-cotton and cotton/polyester T-shirts. Be bold. Experiment with various weaves and knits! Go through the remnant baskets at fabric stores and buy small scraps of cottons, cotton/polyester blends, lightweight polyesters and silks to try out. Keep track of your results, perhaps in a small notebook. How did the pink polyester work with the pastel paints? How did the white satin receive your crisp, fine design? Why did the loveliest bit of silk lose almost all of the pattern the minute you rinsed off the medium? In a sense, you're putting yourself through an extended workshop, and you should approach it with patience and curiosity.

COLLECT COMBS, WHISKS, AND OTHER TOOLS

You'll need tools to apply the paint to the surface, and then other tools to manipulate the colors into a pattern. Tools to drop the paint on the surface include toothpicks, brushes, eyedroppers, atomizers, and small squeeze bottles that allow paint to fall a drop at a time. A whisk can be used to sprinkle a fine mist of color on the surface. To make your own whisk, take about thirty-six straws from a

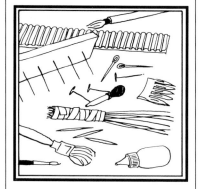

Many marbling tools are common household items; others are easily made.

broom, and cut them to about 6 inches in length. Gather them into a bundle and bind one end with masking tape. To use the whisk, dip it in the paint and flick it over the medium.

Once the paint or ink is on the surface of the medium, you'll need tools to manipulate it into patterns. Any kind of wide-toothed comb will help you produce several of the traditional patterns; Afro picks are a good choice and readily available. We often use the small combs women use to hold back a lock of hair.

Proper marbling combs are nearly the width of the marbling frame. You can make one easily by pushing quilting pins or T-pins through thick cardboard or a wooden lath strip that is 2 inches shorter than the width of the marbling frame, or by stapling those pink plastic hair roller picks from the dime store onto a length of wood or cardboard.

In addition, you will need several small, clean containers with resealable lids (such as baby-food jars) for the mixed paints that you wish to save. Other items you'll need include an ironing board and iron, and embroidery hoops of various sizes. You'll need a stack of 2-inch-wide strips of newspaper because the medium's surface must be cleaned by skimming with paper before you begin and after each print is made.

PREPARE THE MEDIUM

Begin preparation the evening before you intend to marble, as you'll need to let the carrageenan medium rest and thicken for twelve to fourteen hours before you can make the first print. Set up your marbling frame in a place where it can be undisturbed.

We include two recipes, one for heated carrageenan (a slightly coarser powder), the other for blender carrageenan (slightly finer). Both work well. In fact, we can't endorse one over the other, nor can we tell which is which by looking at the finished medium. We include both to ensure that whatever kind of carrageenan you buy, you can use it.

The instructions that follow list several possible sizes of marbling frames with the amount of carrageenan and distilled water they will require. Use these numbers to know how much to buy, then follow the instructions to mix batches until the medium is 1 1/2 to 2 inches deep in the frame. You're going to need a lot; it's easier to handle in small batches.

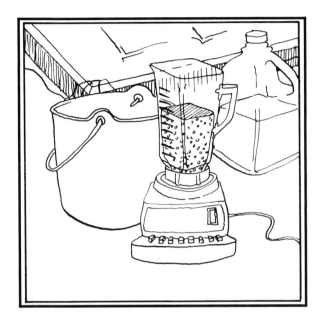

Mix your heated or blender carrageenan according to the recipes on the following pages.

Dimensions		Distilled Water	Carrageenan
Frame	Fabric		
38" x 38"	36" x 36"	7 gallons	1 1/3 cups
20" x 74"	18" x 72"	7 gallons	1 1/3 cups
20" x 38"	18" x 36"	3.5 gallons	2/3 cup
20" x 20"	18" x 18"	1.75 gallons	1/3 cup

1) **Heat 1 quart of distilled water (from a gallon jug) almost to boiling and pour it into a bucket.** Add some of the remaining water from the gallon jug to make a hot-to-the-hands liquid to melt and dissolve the carrageenan.

2) **Sprinkle 1/3 cup or 5 rounded tablespoons of carrageenan into the bucket and stir with a spoon or long stick.** You will notice that while the water does almost immediately get thicker, there are a lot of clumps of carrageenan floating in suspension. Try to break up the larger clumps as you stir. We have found that the best way to break up the remaining clumps is by hand. So roll up your sleeves, and just reach into the gooey stuff and have fun. When you have broken down the bigger lumps, there will still be a bunch of smaller lumps floating about. Don't worry about them; they will dissolve as the medium rests.

Squeeze out the lumps by hand.

3) **Stir in the remainder of the gallon of distilled water.**

4) **Empty the bucket into the frame.** (You did put the liner in, didn't you?)

5) **Repeat steps 1 through 4 until the frame contains 1 1/2 to 2 inches of medium.**

6) **Allow the medium to rest undisturbed for twelve hours or longer.** You can cover the entire frame with a bed sheet or other large cloth to prevent dust and other particles from falling in. Even though the surface will be skimmed with strips of newspaper before beginning to apply colors, it's best to keep the surface as clean as possible. Bubbles and dust will destroy the finest patterns and greatly detract from the appearance of the finished piece. The medium is ready when it is the consistency of light cream and completely clear. Skim it with a strip of newspaper before applying any paint.

BLENDER CARRAGEENAN

Dimensions		Distilled Water	Carrageenan
Frame	Fabric		
38" x 38"	36" x 36"	7 gallons	14 tablespoons
20" x 74"	18" x 72"	7 gallons	14 tablespoons
20" x 38"	18" x 36"	3.5 gallons	7 tablespoons
20" x 20"	18" x 18"	1.75 gallons	3.5 tablespoons

1) **Fill your blender with 1 quart of distilled water and put it on medium speed.** Add 1 level tablespoon of carrageenan to the center of the swirling water and continue to blend for 30 seconds. The mixture will look very thick, whitish and foamy.
2) **Pour the mixture into a bucket. Stir in 1 quart of distilled water.**
3) **Empty the bucket into the frame.**
4) **Repeat these steps until the frame contains 1 1/2 to 2 inches of medium.**

Mix carrageenan in small batches in your blender until the frame is full enough.

5) **Allow the medium to rest undisturbed for at least twelve hours.** Cover it to keep it dust free. When the medium is ready, it will look completely clear and will be almost completely free of small bubbles on the surface. The few bubbles that remain will be skimmed off with strips of newspaper before the first drops of paint are applied.

PREPARE THE FABRIC

The fabric needs some preparation before marbling. The manufacturer's finishing chemicals must be removed, and then alum added to the clean fabric to make it ready to take on the paint and hold it permanently.

1) **Wash the fabric to get rid of any sizing or conditioners added by the manufacturer.** Sizing is what makes new material feel stiff and look new, but it also repels the alum that the fibers must absorb so that the colors will adhere. Fabric that has been treated with a stain repellent will not work for marbling, and neither will water-repellent fabric. After you have washed and thoroughly rinsed the fabric, allow it to dry completely. Use a clothesline, a dryer, or an iron to dry the fabric.

2) **In a large bowl, dissolve 2 tablespoons of alum in 1 quart of warm tap water.** Stir until the alum crystals have disappeared and the solution is only slightly cloudy. We often begin by stirring 8 tablespoons of alum into 1 gallon of water. This solution will keep for many days, and 1 gallon is enough to prepare several yards of fabric or dozens of silk scarves as well as a few T-shirts.

The fabric must be soaked in alum and dried before it will pick up the marbled design.

3) **Drop one piece of fabric at a time into the alum mixture.** Make sure that the fabric is thoroughly soaked. Where there is no alum, there will be no color!

4) **Wring the fabric until no more liquid comes out and hang it to dry.** We recommend drip drying, as a clothes dryer produces static cling that will make the fabric slightly trickier to place on the medium. Using dryer sheets to reduce the static cling can result in unsightly marks. Prepare a full session's worth of fabrics in this alum solution and hang them to dry. Suspend them from pinch-style clothespins rather than folding them over the line so that they will be flat when they are dry.

After a silk scarf has dried, you can hold it up to the light and see any spots of fabric that didn't absorb the alum. The fabric pieces should feel slightly stiff. If insufficient alum was used or the piece was not completely saturated and dried, the color won't hold through rinsing, or some areas will look good while other parts look pale. If you suspect that some of your swatches are not evenly treated with alum, you can soak and dry them again.

5) **Press the fabric with a cool to medium iron (silk setting for silk).** Wrinkles in the cloth will interfere with the

transfer of the pattern to the cloth.

6) **Place your prep[...] near your marl[...]**
We have two o[...] wooden dryir[...] up next to ou[...] times, one witr[...] pressed fabric[...] ble, one or tw[...] ing for newl[...] to be hung f[...]

PREPARE [...]

To work well for mai[...], paint must be able to float and disperse over the top of the medium, yet keep its color distinct from neighboring colors. Some paints will do this just as they come from the bottle, but most must be thinned with something that breaks the surface tension of the paint. We have read that dish detergent or Photo-Flo (from a photography store) will work for this, but we have not been successful with either of those products. We recommend thinning with water and a little oxgall.

It's a good idea to test the paint in a shallow bowl of medium first. Be sure to use the largest bowl possible. A small cup of medium will have a different surface tension, and will not accurately demonstrate how the paint will behave over a larger surface area.

1) **Open the vials of paint and mix the colors you want in a** small cup, about 2 tablespoons of each mixed color.

2) **Test the paint by placing 1 drop on the surface of the medium.** If the paint is the proper consistency, it will float on the surface and spread slowly out from the center of the drop in a uniform pattern to form a circle 2 to 4 inches in diameter. If it is too thick, the paint will either sink to the bottom of the medium or stay in a glob on the surface without dispersing. If the paint is too thin, it will disperse very quickly and be so pale as to be difficult to see on the surface of the medium.

3) **Adjust the consistency of the paint.** If the paint is too thick, place one drop of oxgall in the mixed paint, using an eyedropper, and stir. Test again. If you haven't any oxgall, you can thin the paints with plain water and achieve reasonably good results. For thick paints, thin with tap water and a couple of drops of oxgall.

If the paint is too thin, it can still be used. Drop the thin color on the medium first, then crowd the surface of the medium with other colors that are the proper consistency. When the surface is crowded with paint, the thin areas are pushed into smaller, brighter bands of color.

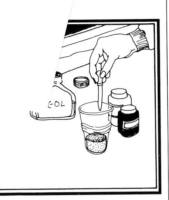

If the paint is too thick, add a drop of oxgall.

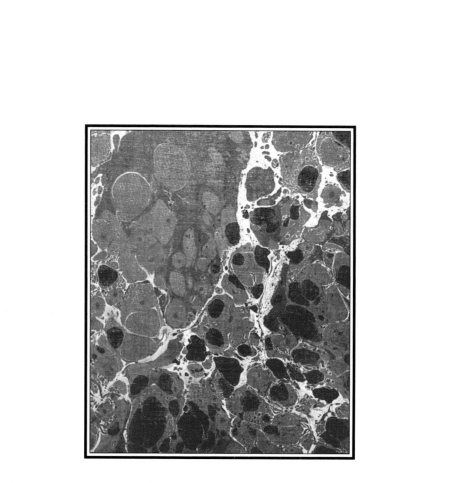

Turkish Traditional Pattern

*You are
now ready
to begin
the fun . . .*

After the medium has rested for twelve hours, most of the bubbles will be gone and the medium will look clear except for a few tiny bubbles on the surface. Skim off those bubbles with a strip of newspaper held upright and pulled toward you across the surface of the medium. Discard the strip.

Having prepared the medium, prepared the fabric, and prepared and laid out your paints, you are now ready to begin the fun part.

APPLY THE PAINT

Using a brush, chopstick, whisk, or eyedropper, gently drop paint on the surface of the medium. If you move too quickly, or drop paints from too far above the medium, you'll likely find most of your paints on the bottom of the frame, beyond use.

The height from which the paint can be dropped depends on the size of the drops. If you

*Drop paint until the surface of
the medium is covered.*

are using a broomstraw whisk, the drops will be fine, so you can hold the whisk as high as 12 to 18 inches above the medium. If you are using a chopstick, the drop will be so large that it will sink to the bottom of the medium unless the stick is held immediately above or just touching the medium. Other applicators will be best held at some point between these extremes.

Continue adding drops of paint until you are satisfied that there is enough on the surface of the medium. Don't be discouraged when paint falls to the bottom of the frame. This is unavoidable. Experience will guide you in thinning the paint and placing it so that it remains on the surface.

MAKE THE PATTERN

When the surface is full of color, it's ready for you to manipulate into any number of beautiful patterns. On the following pages are several patterns as a starting point. We have given these patterns common names, but you'll find as you read more about marbling that there is little consistency in naming patterns. Our version of bouquet, for example, is not the same as the bouquet that appears on page 88.

There are many more design possibilities beyond these few. We hope that you will study the books on paper marbling listed in the Bibliography; there you'll find photos of old and new patterns with instructions for creating them, including the patterns shown at our chapter openings.

To make your chosen pattern, comb the paint as described on the following pages.

LAY THE FABRIC

Once you're satisfied with the design on your medium, pick up the alum-treated cloth by each of the four corners. It helps greatly, and is much more fun also, to do this step with another person. Holding the cloth over the medium, carefully check where it will hit the pattern. (Once the cloth is down on the medium, you won't be able to move it without destroying the design.) Then slowly drop the middle of the fabric so that it contacts the surface of the medium first. Smoothly drop the balance of the material so that the corners and outside edges come into contact last. Most fabrics become translucent

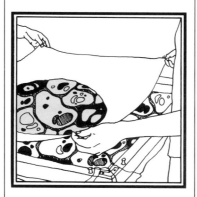

Drop the fabric smoothly onto the surface of patterned paint.

when wet, so you will be able to see the pattern through the fabric. If there are areas where the fabric has bubbled up and is not in contact with the medium, gently press them down with your hand until the material touches the paint pattern.

It is also possible to lay the fabric on the medium with just two hands. If the fabric is small, spread one hand along each of two opposite sides and lower the center loose fold first, then slowly lower each side. If the fabric is large, hold two adjacent corners and lower the free-hanging edge into the marbling bath at the far side of the frame, then lower the fabric toward yourself.

LIFT, RINSE, AND DRY THE FABRIC

When you see that the fabric has taken on the paint, you are ready for a messy but highly rewarding step. Grab two adjacent corners of the fabric and lift it out of the medium. You should now be breathless. Even though we've marbled many pieces of material, we are still as wide-eyed as children when we see the result of our work. As the fabric is raised out of the frame, it will drip medium and some paint will slide off. Don't panic. Hold the fabric over a drip bucket and proceed to the nearest sink. Rinse the fabric under cool running water until it loses the slippery feeling of the carrageenan. Don't scrub or scrape, though. If there are tiny areas that seem to have a glob of paint, rinse well under running water but don't touch with your fingers. Leave the spot until the fabric dries or else you're likely to smear the small bit into the wet fabric in an unpredictable and disappointing way and thus destroy the edges of pattern next to it. Hang the rinsed fabric on a clothesline.

Look closely at the fabric on the clothesline. If it has crinkled marks where the paint has partially rubbed off, you'll know to handle the other pieces of this fabric by using a plastic-covered sheet of cardboard to carry them from the marbling bath to the sink and then to the clothesline. On some fabrics, especially slick-surfaced synthetics, the paint is rather delicate when it is wet, so it needs to be prevented from rubbing against itself until it is dry and ironed.

Allow the fabric to dry completely before removing it from the clothesline. Let the dried fabric rest undisturbed for at least 3 days, then either steam press with a household iron or tumble the fabric in a hot clothes dryer for a half hour. This resting and heating sets the colors so they will be permanent. Ready-made silk ties marbled with acrylic paints can rest for three days and then be heated with a steam iron held away

To clean and reduce the surface tension of the medium so it is ready for the next print, skim it with strips of newspaper.

from the surface so the soft-fold edges are not flattened.

SKIM THE MEDIUM

After you marble one piece of fabric, some paint will remain on the surface of the medium. Skim it by drawing a few strips of newspaper across it before applying paints for the next piece of fabric. One application of paint prints one piece of fabric, and the frame must be skimmed after each print.

CLEAN UP

If the medium has been used only a few times and is still quite clear and you don't think you'll be using it again for several days, you can add a few drops of formaldehyde (from your local pharmacy), empty the medium into clean gallon jugs, and store it in a cool area until you need it again. If you don't have formaldehyde on hand, just pour it into clean jugs and refrigerate for as long as two weeks.

When carrageenan sits too long or in too warm a place, it develops mold. A foul odor is the tip that it is time to discard it.

The carrageenan medium in a large frame will last for seven days or longer. Some of the medium evaporates and some is removed with each piece of fabric, and eventually the whole thing becomes too murky and thick to work on. If you can't clearly see the paints on the surface because of the stuff floating midway down, it's time to bail out and begin again.

If you have a very large marbling frame, you will need to bail it out by dipping a cup at a time into either the sink or a clean jug. Whether you pour or dip to remove the medium, if you plan to save it to reuse you will want to transfer it in as clear a state as possible. Try not to disturb the droplets of paint that have collected on the bottom. Remove the bottom quarter-inch of medium by rinsing it down the drain, thus throwing away most of the color pollution. Since acrylic paints are nontoxic and carrageenan is a food product, they do not need special care in disposal.

If your medium is clean enough to save for another project, scoop it into gallon jugs.

CARE OF MARBLED FABRICS

After you have dried, rested, and ironed your marbled fabrics, treat them as you would a fine sweater: gently hand wash or dry clean. If your washing machine has a silk basket and a gentle cycle, fine. Avoid hot water and your regular detergents, which are just too harsh. We once threw several lovely T-shirts in with our favorite heavy-duty liquid detergent and a load of the kids' clothes and were chagrined to find that 50 percent of the marbled color went down the drain.

On the other hand, we have washed marbled cotton/polyester blend sheets and unbleached 100 percent cotton muslin shirts right in with the regular laundry and not lost any color. With these fabrics, we recommend that you run a few test swatches through all the steps from printing, to drip drying, to resting for three days, to machine washing and see what happens. Better to lose a nice design that's only on a 4-inch by 8-inch swatch than on a finished garment.

Steam press the fabrics on the wrong side if needed.

COLOR MIXING

While acrylic paints come in many colors, you can make your own personal color palette by mixing the basic colors. Start with clear blue, process blue (turquoise-blue), warm red (orange-red), cool red (purplish red), yellow, black, and white.

The following formulas are meant to serve as general guidelines for achieving some popular hues. The most wonderful color magic will happen as you play around with adding a drop of one thing or another to a basic mixture. Don't be afraid to experiment.

OLIVE	15 parts yellow 1 part process blue 2 parts black	PLUM	10 parts cool red 4 parts blue drop of black	PEACH	1 part yellow 1 part warm red 30 parts white
TEAL	14 parts process blue 1 part yellow drop of black	RUST	12 parts yellow 4 parts cool red drop of black	PINK	1 part warm red 1 part cool red 14 parts white
GREEN	3 parts process blue 1 part yellow	GOLD	16 parts yellow drop warm red drop black	MINT	1 part yellow 3 parts process blue 60 parts white
MAUVE	5 parts green 3 parts warm red	WALNUT	6 parts cool red 2 parts blue 8 parts yellow 1 part black	LIME	4 parts yellow 28 parts white 1/4 part process blue
WINE	13 parts warm red 3 parts process blue	TAN	1 part cool red 3 parts yellow 28 parts white		

ONE

Adjust the surface tension of the medium by skimming it with newspaper immediately before you begin, then drop your prepared paints on the surface using any of the tools you've collected. Crowd the surface with paint in order to keep the colors bright and clear.

TWO

Comb the paint into any of the patterns shown on the next pages. The fabric will look exactly like the surface of the medium, so work with the design until you are happy with it. An unsatisfactory design can be skimmed off and thrown away.

THREE

In a slow, fluid motion, lay the prepared fabric on the marbled surface. Any pause or jerk will disturb the pattern, so make this a smooth motion. Pause a few moments to let the pattern soak into the fabric.

FOUR

Lift the fabric by two corners and, holding it as flat as possible, gently rinse it under running water. The wet paint surface is delicate so do not let the marbled side of the fabric rub on itself.

FIVE

Using clip clothespins, hang the fabric to dry so that it does not rub against any other surface. Allow it to dry completely, then let it rest for three days. After three days, iron the fabric to further set the design. It can then be gently hand washed.

SIX

Skim the surface of the medium with strips of newspaper to remove any paint residue and to prepare it for the next marbled design.

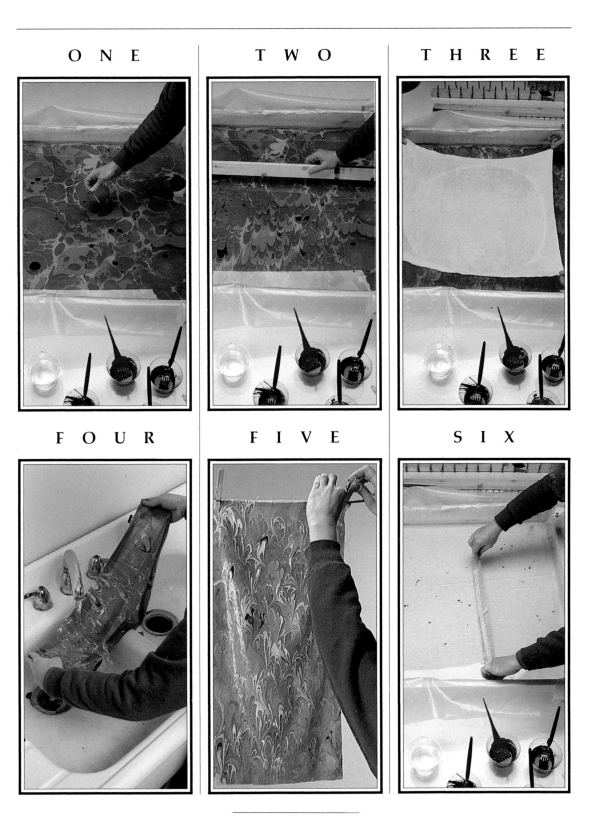

O N E

T W O

T H R E E

F O U R

F I V E

S I X

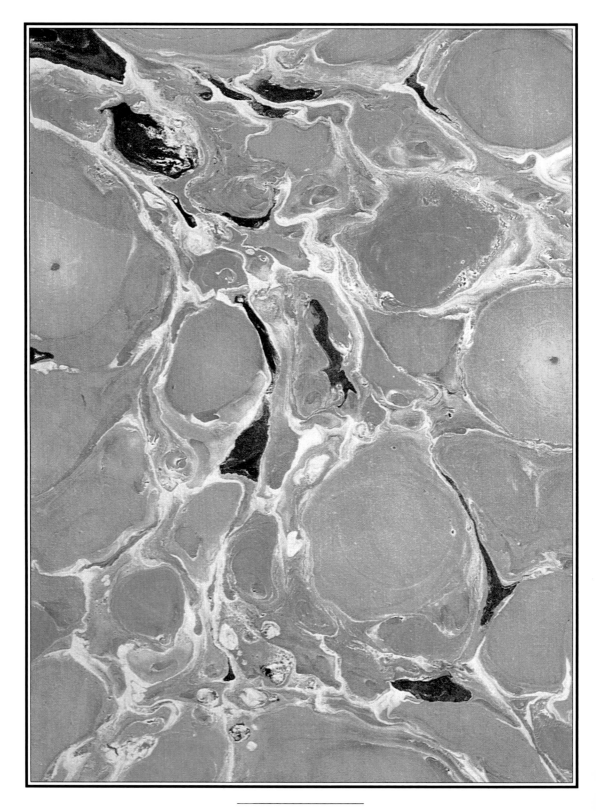

S T O N E

To create the stone pattern, cover the surface of the medium with drops of color, not combing, mixing, or swirling them in any way. This resembles the natural patterns sometimes found in marble.

F R E E S T Y L E

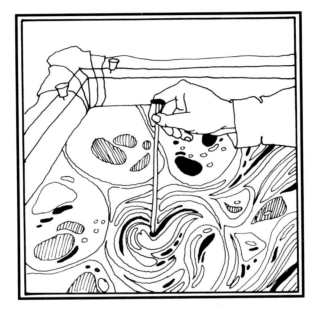

For a freestyle pattern, cover the surface with drops of color and then draw them into random swirls with a chopstick, toothpick or other stylus. Insert the stylus into the medium so that it barely penetrates the surface of the medium. As you slowly draw the stylus through one color of paint into another, bands of color are formed. Or do freestyle work with your stylus after creating a combed design as this photograph shows. Combed pattern is described on the next page.

C O M B E D

Many designs start with a combed pattern. Beginning with the stone pattern, use a marbling comb (see page 20) or a small hair comb such as an Afro pick to draw slowly and shallowly along the length of the frame. Comb the entire surface with parallel strokes. To get a finer mix of color with the combed pattern, comb again at right angles to the first combing. The more you repeat this process, the finer the color areas become.

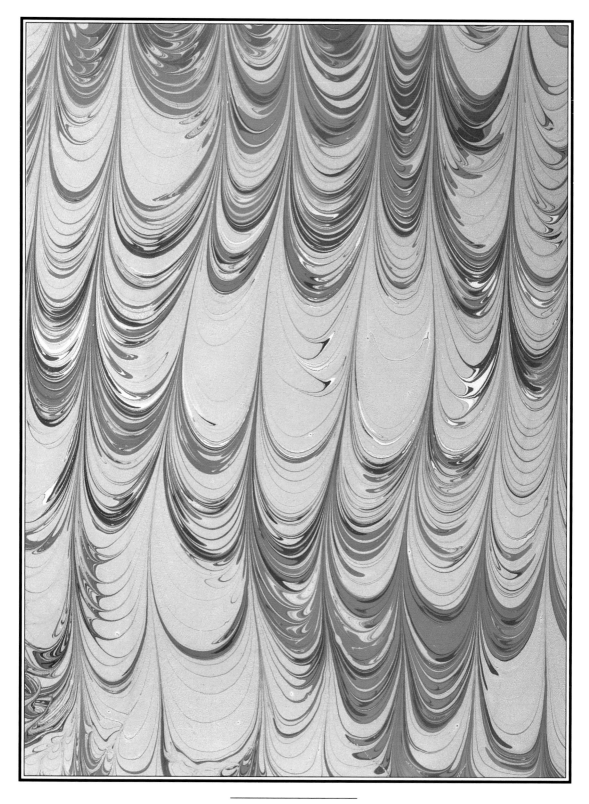

To make a cascade pattern, begin with a combed pattern. Use a stylus to draw lines at right angles to the combed lines, all going in the same direction and about an inch apart.

Nonpareil is very similar to cascade except that it is finer. Make a cascade pattern with more closely spaced lines, all drawn in the same direction.

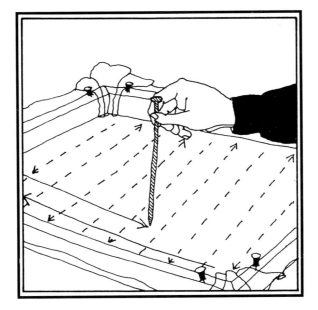

The feather pattern also begins with a combed design. Comb the colors into parallel lines and then go back with a stylus and draw slowly through, perpendicular to the first combing, with lines going in alternate directions from edge to edge, moving over about an inch with each succeeding line.

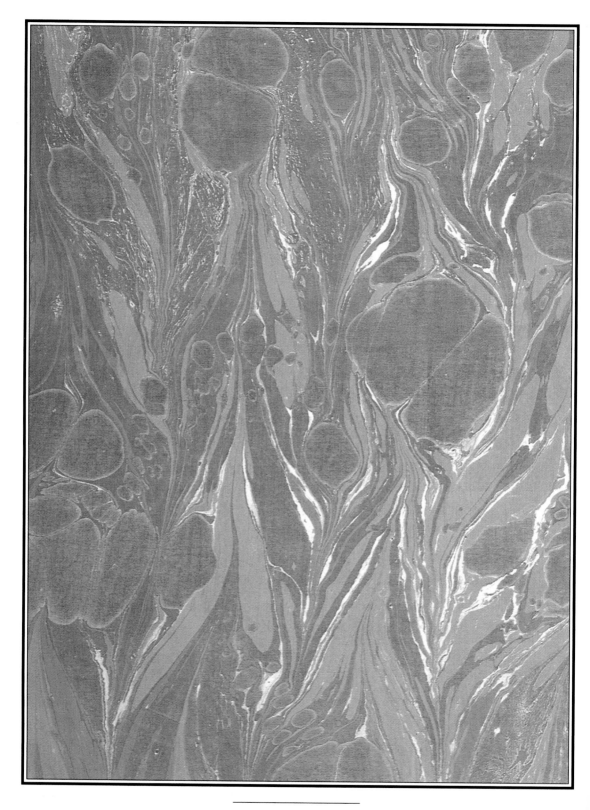

This spots-on-stripes design doesn't really resemble a zebra. Apply tiny droplets of paint with a whisk over a feather pattern, causing dots of color to form at random over the controlled design.

B O U Q U E T

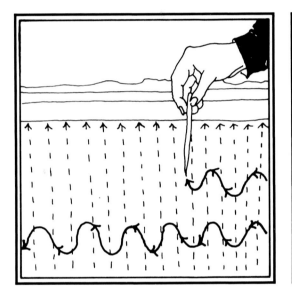 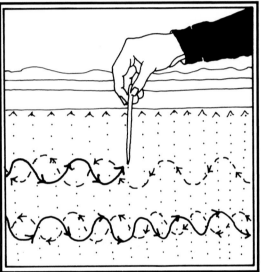

Bouquet is a complex-looking design that is easy to make. Begin with a fine combed pattern. Draw parallel S curves, at right angles to the combed design. Then draw another set of S curves in the opposite direction and offset to form figure eights.

WINGS

Wings pattern is named for the path of the stylus rather than the look of the finished design. Make it by drawing the stylus parallel to a combed design in a lopsided scallop pattern like a column of wings, half hearts, or bass clefs.

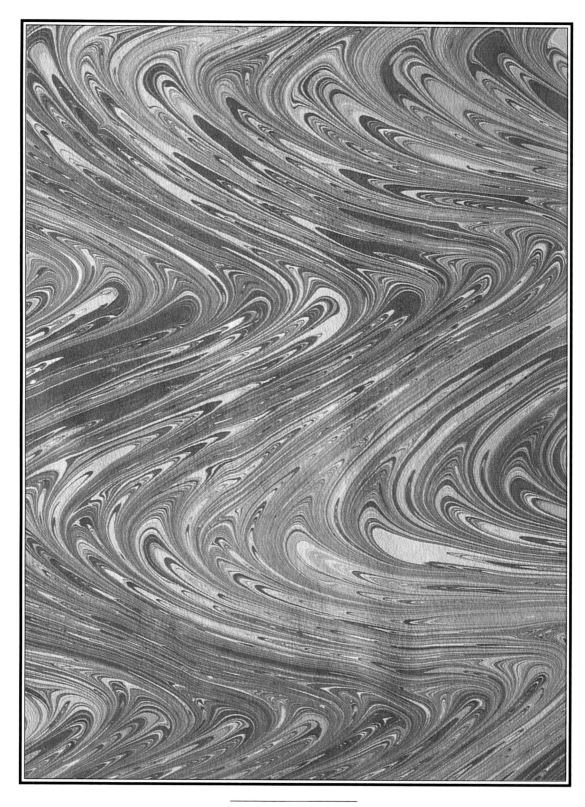

W A V E

"Wave" really describes the look of this design. Begin with a fine combed pattern. Using a marbling comb that is 2 inches shorter than the width of your frame, draw a series of W's across the surface, bumping the edges of the frame at each change of direction.

Shadow marbling, or over-marbling, is not a traditional named pattern but is a handsome technique nevertheless. It involves printing, rinsing, drying, re-aluming, and printing again for an effect of one pattern superimposed on another.

Throw pillows are an excellent first project. Because you can print many squares of fabric and then choose only your favorites to make into pillows, there is little lost if a few squares are disappointing.

As you buy white or light-colored material for this project, remember that a smooth fabric will show the design better than a more textured one. You'll probably want a somewhat substantial fabric for this use, rather than a softly draping type. We used a bleached muslin. Wait to buy the backing fabric, as matching will be easier if you marble first and buy coordinating fabric afterwards.

Machine wash and dry your fabric. Cut it into 18-inch squares and soak them in a solution of 8 tablespoons of alum per gallon of warm tap water. Hang to line dry. When they're completely dry and ironed, stack

THROW PILLOWS

As an introduction to marbling, try printing squares of fabric and then making your most successful ones into decorative pillows.

the pieces close to your marbling frame.

Mix your colors, thinning with water and oxgall until they have the proper consistency (see page 25). Be patient; this is an essential step. When the paints are right, drop them on the medium and manipulate them into any of the patterns shown on pages 34 to 55.

We used the same colors to make four different patterns for our set of four pillows. We began with the stone pattern, simply dropping paint on the medium until we liked the design. The cascade and feathered designs both began as combed patterns, combed several times horizontally to form stripes of color. For the cascade pattern, we drew a toothpick (you could use any kind of stylus) at right angles to the combed stripes, making all draws in the same direction and about an inch apart. The feather design is similar except that we drew the stylus across the combed stripes with an up-down-up-down motion.

To make the wave pattern, we made a marbling comb 2 inches narrower than the frame by stapling plastic hairpins an inch apart on a 1-inch by 2-inch wooden stick. We placed paint as before and made a fine combed design. Then, working in the same direction as the combed design, we moved the rake in a wavy line, bumping the edge of the frame each time we changed direction (see page 53).

When you have made a design you like on your medium, lay a prepared fabric square carefully on the surface. Watch for a few seconds as the fabric absorbs some moisture and the design. Since the fabric becomes translucent as it gets wet, this is easy to see. Hold two adjacent corners of the fabric and lift it off the medium. Use the drip bucket to carry the fabric to the sink. Rinse it well under cold running water and then hang to line dry.

Look closely at the surface of this first marbled print. If there are spots where the paint rubbed off during the rinsing, use a plastic-covered cardboard tray to carry the next marbled pieces from the marbling bath to the sink and then to the clothesline. A few fabrics do not hold the paint very firmly until

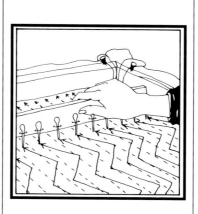

To make the wave pattern, move the marbling rake back and forth in a zigzag style as described on page 53.

they are dry and pressed; these fabrics need to be handled flat until they dry so that areas of wet paint don't rub against each other.

Skim your marbling bath with strips of newspaper to remove the paint that was left behind so that it is clean for the next design. Make more designs following this procedure. You can mix different colors for each design, or do as we did and make the pillows look like a set by using the same colors for all of them.

When the fabric squares are completely dry, put them away for three days and then iron them on the wrong side. If they are still a little stiffer than the original cloth, you can hand wash them and again let them dry and iron them.

Now go buy the fabric for the backs. Or, if you prefer, use another marbled square for the back. Place the two squares right sides together, with or without piping or ruffle trim, and sew around three sides and part of the fourth. Turn right side out and stuff with polyester fiberfill or a ready-made 18-inch pillow form. Pillows made with ready-made forms will look better if the cover is slightly smaller than the form so that the pillow looks tightly stuffed. Neatly sew the opening closed by hand and display your designer pillows proudly.

OTHER IDEAS

There are many other small projects you can make with the other good prints from this series—glasses cases, small book covers, or even a marbled marble bag.

We recently made a series of rainbow-striped scarves by dropping paints in bands. On the far left of the frame we placed deep purple drops in a straight line top to bottom, then a string of white, then indigo, then white, moving each successive band of color 2 or 3 inches to the right, through green, white, yellow, white, orange, white, red. Some drifting occurred, but in general, this made a rainbow-stripe effect. Then we combed, feathered, cascaded, or waved the paint before printing.

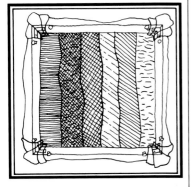

For a rainbow-striped effect, drop the paint in lines of color before you begin to comb the design.

Why not a marbled marble bag with one of your small pieces of marbled fabric?

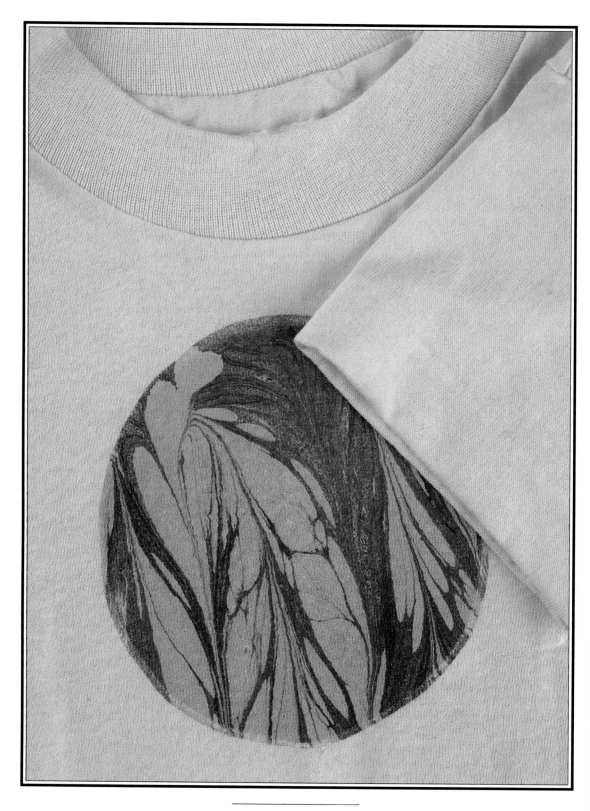

For your first attempts with T-shirts, we recommend buying cotton/polyester shirts, three to a package at your local dime store. White or light-colored shirts will show the design best. You'll also need an embroidery hoop the size of the circle you want to make. Plastic embroidery hoops work better than wooden ones because the wood tends to absorb some of the moisture and paint, and then the edges of the marbled circle are not quite smooth.

Machine wash the T-shirts on a regular cycle with warm to hot water and a laundry detergent that does not contain fabric softener. Put the shirts through a second rinse cycle to remove all detergent residue. Line dry or tumble dry on low heat but without using any fabric softener sheets.

T-SHIRT WITH A CIRCULAR MOTIF

T-shirts are terrific with swirly marbled patterns. Printing a single isolated area makes the project extremely fast and easy.

When the shirts are dry, soak them well in a solution of 8 tablespoons of alum dissolved in 1 gallon of warm water. Line dry the shirts.

We've printed a marbled design only in the center of the chest on this shirt. Place a plastic embroidery hoop in the spot where you want the design to appear. Holding back all portions of the shirt except the area in the hoop, gently lower only the circle onto the medium. Be careful to barely touch the medium with the stretched surface so that the paint does not go up into the small opening in the outer hoop. Keeping the printed area lower than the rest of the shirt, immerse it in cold water and gently remove the hoop. Rinse the shirt well. If paint has run up into the gap in the outer hoop, making a little nub of unwanted color on your otherwise perfect circular design, use your fingernail to scrape it off as you rinse the shirt. Then into the dryer it goes, and voilà! You've created a one-of-a-kind T-shirt.

ANOTHER IDEA

Rather than marbling only a circular area, you can print the entire T-shirt. Prepare the shirt by washing, drying, soaking in alum, and line drying, as described above.

When it's completely dry, stretch the T-shirt over a cardboard or styrofoam T-shirt insert. Many craft stores now carry such inserts, or you can cut your own from materials you have on hand. If you're planning to do several shirts, you may want to either cover the cardboard insert with plastic or have it laminated.

When you are satisfied with the marbled pattern in your frame, center the T-shirt over it, holding steadily at the neck and hem edges of the insert. Gently lower the T-shirt onto the medium and push down slightly so the paints flow up the narrow edge of the cardboard but not across the back of the shirt. Lift it off.

With the T-shirt stretched over a cardboard form, print one side first.

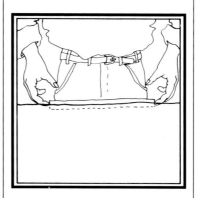

Push the cardboard form down slightly so that the marbled design comes up the sides of the T-shirt.

Stand the T-shirt on edge to drip over newspapers while you skim the medium and create a similar design for the back of the shirt. Dip the back as you did the front, pushing down each edge until the pattern on the back meets the pattern on the front, so that no unprinted areas are left at the sides and the shoulders. If the back of the shirt has remained dry right up to the edge where the pattern was applied to the front, this second dip will not overdye the first dip because the wet area will resist further paint while the dry area will accept it.

Note, however, that if the back of the shirt got wet when you marbled the front, it will not take the paint on the second dip. In that case you must rinse and dry the shirt and re-apply alum, insert the cardboard again, and then print the back.

After both sides have been printed, carefully remove the shirt from the insert and rinse it thoroughly in cool running water. Dry the shirt in a dryer on high heat to set the colors. Launder separately in cold water the first time or two, though none of the paint should run off the T-shirt after heat setting in the dryer.

A T-shirt with an all-over design is a bit harder than one with a single spot of design, but it certainly is dramatic.

Though we are primarily fabric marblers, we've had fun making marbled papers for greeting cards or note cards. Buy a smooth-textured paper of the thickness you want. If it is bigger than your marbling frame, use a paper cutter or sharp knife to cut it to size. Soak the paper in the alum solution, using a shallow rectangular pan so you don't crumple it. Dry it completely, then press with a steam iron to flatten it. If the paper is not flat, it will be difficult to enter it smoothly into the marbling bath, and you will get an uneven print. Dip the alum-treated, ironed paper as you would fabric, trying not to let the painted design run across the back of the paper. Hang to dry, leave for three days, and steam iron from the back side to flatten the paper again. Buy colored envelopes,

NOTE CARDS

Catch the bits of design around your other projects or print big sheets of marbled paper for cards, stationery, or bookmarks.

and then use a paper cutter or sharp knife to trim the paper to fit them.

OTHER IDEAS

We've had fun catching small bits of pattern left on the sides of the tank with alum-treated, unlined 3-inch by 5-inch cards. At holiday time, our children have made simple Christmas ornaments by tracing cookie cutter shapes onto the marbled cards, cutting them out, stringing thread or ribbon through a hole at the top, and then spraying lightly all over with gold or silver spray glitter.

Marbling wooden shapes is also easy and fun. They can be used for jewelry or holiday ornaments. At most craft stores you'll find a wide variety of small wooden shapes for sale, either loose in bins to pick and choose, or smaller bits prepackaged by the hundreds. We handle these the same way as fabric or paper: alum, dry, and dip, then rest for three days. We have used wooden stars, hearts and ovals, marbling on one side, painting solid color on the other, and then gluing on either a loop for hanging or a pin back for wearing as jewelry. Clear acrylic spray glaze makes a shiny, attractive finish for the marbled side.

Another project using wood is shown on page 75.

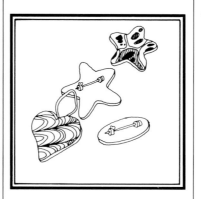

Marble small wooden forms for jewelry or decorations.

Use the scraps from your note-card project for bookmarks or gift tags. A small hole with a bit of ribbon strung through is a nice finishing touch.

Marbling on tissue paper feels a lot like marbling on cloth because the paper is so flexible. Handle the tissue paper like the heavier note-card paper. The successful large pieces make beautiful wrapping paper, and smaller pieces can be glued to the front of a heavier, solid-color note card.

*Hand-marbled bookmarks of heavy paper, trimmed with a bit
of ribbon, make good gifts.*

PIECED JACKET

This is a great way to make marbled clothing if your work space is too small for a huge frame, or if you would like to combine different marbled designs in the same garment. Start with a simple garment shape like this jacket from Simplicity pattern 8540. For the marbled areas, buy white fabric such as silk broadcloth. Marble as many designs as you wish on pieces of the white fabric, using the same colors in each piece. While your marbled pieces are resting for three days, buy a solid-color fabric that coordinates with your marbling colors. We chose raw silk. The pieced marbled sections are appliquéd onto the jacket pieces, rather than replacing any of them, so buy all the materials called for by the pattern. After three days, steam press the marbled pieces to heat set the colors, and steam press the coor-

Here's an exciting way to use your scraps, samples, and experiments: piece them into a high-fashion jacket.

dinating fabric to preshrink it. Pencil in lines on the pattern envelope picture of the garment as you plan the piecing.

Cut and sew together pieces of your marbled fabrics, creating a design from any traditional quilting pattern or from your own imagination. Cut out the front and back sections of your pattern, and appliqué this pieced design in place. Assemble the rest of the jacket according to the pattern instructions.

OTHER IDEAS

Add a freeform appliqué to any garment, using bits of coordinating fabric and decorative machine zigzag stitching.

Rather than using your marbled fabric as an appliquéd accent, you can piece an entire garment using marbled and coordinated fabrics. Sew marbled fabric and solid fabric together to make a pieced rectangle of fabric for each front section, the back, and each sleeve. Then use a commercial pattern to cut the actual jacket sections from these rectangles.

Decorative pillows, quilts, and other kinds of clothing are excellent uses for your small swatches of marbled cloth. Follow any of the traditional or contemporary quilting designs or make up your own. Hand-marbled fabrics can be used in conjunction with other craft techniques to make beautiful and dramatic one-of-a-kind clothing, quilts and wall-hangings. Try embroidery, appliqué, quilting through a marbled pattern to enhance the painted detail, or outlining and highlighting with metallic paints brushed on later.

Construct modular clothing such as a simple gathered skirt from squares or rectangles of fabric sewn together, hemming one end and gathering with elastic at the other. For fit, take your hip measurement and add 8 to

Sketch your design ideas on the pattern envelope as you plan your pieced appliqué.

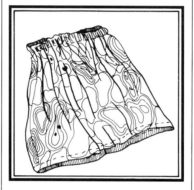

Two rectangles of fabric, with elastic at the top and a hem at the bottom, make an attractive modular skirt.

Two marbled silk scarves make a simple blouse to wear belted or loose.

10 inches. This is how wide your fabric needs to be. Now measure from your waist to your desired hem length, and add 3 inches. This will give you 1 1/2 inches to turn down for the elastic waistband and a 1 1/2-inch hem at the bottom. Marble first and sew your matching marbled squares or rectangles together until you have a rectangle of these measurements. Sew the side seams, make a casing at the top and insert elastic, and hem the skirt.

Or make a simple oversized modular blouse from two 36-inch-square marbled silk scarves. Right sides together, place one on the other and at the top mark a center neck opening at least 12 inches wide with silk pins. Sew each shoulder seam from the pin to the edge of the scarf. Leaving 6-inch slits at the bottom, sew the side seams up to about 10 inches below the shoulder seam. Turn the blouse right side out and wear loose or belted.

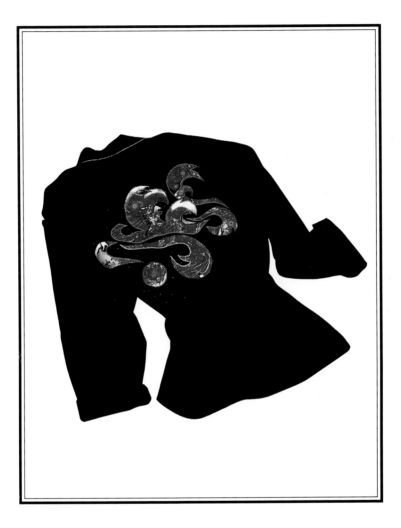

Add a freeform appliqué to ready-made or hand-sewn clothing for a simple but dramatic personal touch.

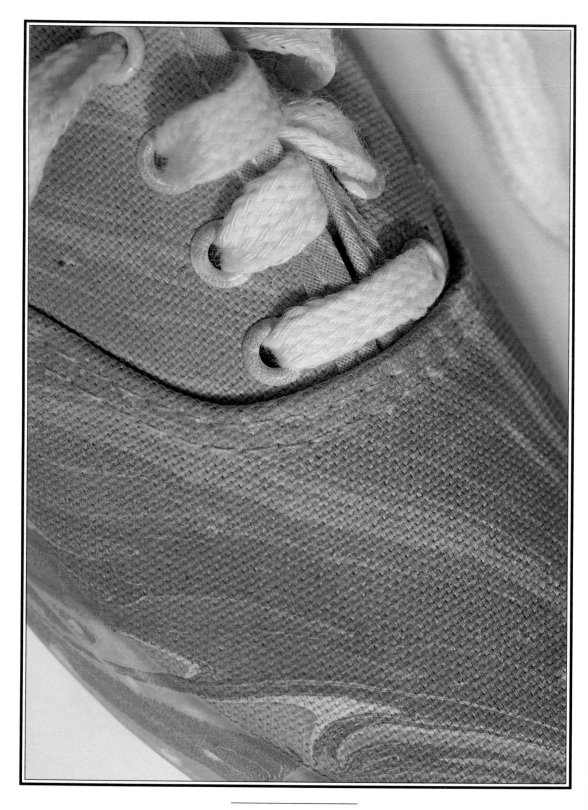

CANVAS TENNIS SHOES

Canvas tennis shoes provide a canvas for your artistry. Buy inexpensive tennis shoes or deck shoes with a smooth upper, one size larger than you normally wear to allow for shrinkage. Do not launder them. Soak the shoes in a solution of 2 tablespoons of alum and 1 quart of warm water, and allow them to dry completely.

Make a marbled pattern with acrylic paints on your medium. The medium should have a surface at least 18 by 24 inches to do both shoes in a similar pattern. Hold a dry shoe upside down with your thumb and fingertips grasping just at the rubber edge of the sole, in the middle of the shoe. Starting on one edge of the medium, tilt the shoe to its outside edge, and gently roll it in the marbling medium from the outer edge of the frame toward the center until the paints have swirled completely around the shoe. Repeat in the opposite direction (again side to center) for the other shoe. If you're brave, and you want them to look as much alike as possible, take a shoe in each hand and work from the edges toward the center of the marbling frame, rolling both shoes at the same time. Rinse thoroughly and allow the shoes to air dry, then run the dry shoes in a hot dryer for half an hour to heatset the colors. You can wear them as soon as they come out of the dryer, but don't wash them for at least three days.

Marbled tennis shoes make a zingy fashion statement; producing them will teach you how to marble any three-dimensional object.

OTHER IDEAS

Baby slippers, satin house shoes, and light-colored suede shoes can all be marbled this way. Keep in mind that you're not just working on the surface, but actually rolling the shoe along somewhat under the surface. This means you may encounter some air bubbles and end up with spots that didn't get any paint at all. You can let them dry, reapply alum, and marble that spot again, or shadow marble. Or you can take small sponge pieces dipped in paints and try dabbing paint in the missed spots and elsewhere for a secondary effect. Take a playful attitude and try other fun techniques like going back over the marbled pattern with felt-tip markers, fabric-paint markers, metallic pencils, stencils, spray-ons, or stick-ons.

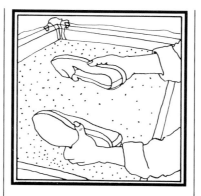

When you are happy with the design on your medium, roll the prepared tennis shoes through the paint pattern, from the outside toward the center of the marbling frame.

Marble a canvas book bag by holding it with paper towel rolls as you dip and turn it.

Try marbling other purchased, three-dimensional objects with this technique. A canvas book bag is an easy project. Either use a cardboard insert to help hold it flat, or use cardboard paper towel rolls held inside each end of the bag to dip it, pushing downward slightly to get paint up and over the side seams. Then either roll the bag to marble the other side (as you did for the tennis shoes) or lift and re-dip (as for the second side of the fully-marbled T-shirt).

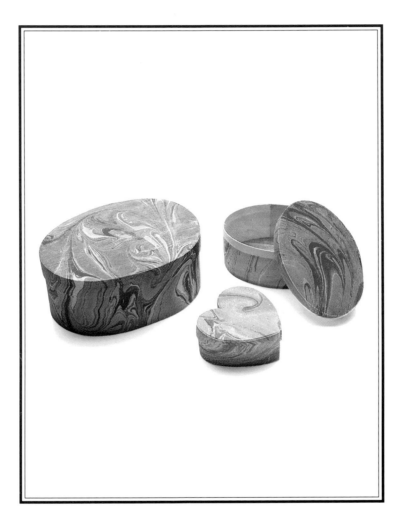

Marie Palowoda marbled these Shaker boxes with their lids in place so that the design flows smoothly from the top to the sides.

SILK KIMONO

While it is possible to buy ready-made white clothing and wash, dry, alum, dry, and marble it, there are several drawbacks to this process. First, there's no guarantee that ready-made items don't contain permanent press agents or stain repellents that will inhibit marbling. Second, a constructed blouse is a more complex shape than a T-shirt or a tennis shoe, so it will have to be printed as many as three times to be patterned all over, including all the seam areas. This is time-consuming, challenging, and risky; if the back doesn't come out looking much like the front, you're stuck with it, or you'll have to consider a second process such as shadow marbling or adding hand-painted accents in contrasting colors to try to pull the garment together as a more unified whole. If you really do want to marble a ready-made blouse, we recommend that you follow the steps as outlined for T-shirts using an insert.

We think, though, that you'd do much better to buy yardage in cotton, cotton/polyester blend, or silk. Wash, dry, and press the yardage and then cut out pieces using your favorite skirt, blouse, dress, or pants pattern. Alum the cut pieces, dry, and then marble them. Plan ahead, thinking through the colors and marbled designs you want, and anticipating which way the fabric pieces will need to be placed so that the marbled patterns will fit together well. When the marbled pieces have been rinsed, dried, rested for three days and pressed again, sew the article together as the pattern describes.

Though it takes some sewing skill, one advantage of this

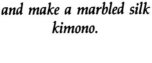

For the ultimate in elegance, build an extra large frame and make a marbled silk kimono.

method is that the seams of the finished garments don't have any white streaks where no marbling occurred. Another is that you can see before sewing how well all the parts interact, and make corrections by cutting and marbling a replacement piece.

We made this silk charmeuse kimono by this method with New Look pattern 6312. We needed a marbling frame slightly bigger than the largest pattern piece; since we planned to have a center back seam, a front panel would be our largest piece. We measured the length and width of the front pattern piece, added 1 inch on each side, and built a rectangular frame of that size with lumber, metal corner angles, and a clear plastic drop cloth.

We ordered silk charmeuse fabric from one of the suppliers listed on page 91. We cut out the pattern pieces and prepared each of the front, back, and sleeve pieces with alum. We mixed the paints and tested them, making sure we had plenty of each mixed color for all of the panels. A project this big takes a surprising amount of paint, perhaps as much as 2 ounces of each mixed color. Recreating a similar pattern six times was an interesting challenge as we tried to make two front panels, two back panels, and two sleeves look alike.

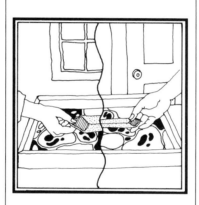

Use a long, narrow frame with one person at each end to marble ready-made silk ties.

After we had printed, dried, rested, and steam pressed each piece, we simply sewed the kimono as the pattern directed.

OTHER IDEAS

Silk scarves and ties are also great to marble. We buy hand-hemmed white silk scarves and white silk twill neckties through one or another of the mail-order fabric companies listed on page 91. Because these silk scarves and ties are made for hand decorating, they don't contain sizing or other chemicals. So we don't machine wash them, but put them directly into an alum solution until they're saturated. We gently squeeze out the excess solution and hang them to dry. The ties need no further preparation, but the scarves usually require ironing on silk setting to remove wrinkles.

Ties and long, narrow scarves are most easily done in a frame we've built especially for them, which measures 18 by 72 inches. With a person at each end of the frame holding the edges of the necktie above the marbled pattern, we gently and evenly lower the tie onto the paint. With fingertips or a stylus, we then gently push the tie just below the surface, forcing the color to flow up over its rounded sides and giving it a more completely marbled appearance.

If you're working in a smaller frame, you'll have to marble the tie in sections, or plan to marble only a small area here and there and be careful to alum and dip only those sections where pattern is desired.

To marble the prehemmed cotton scarves from India that are sold by these suppliers, we recommend washing them first and then proceeding as usual with drying, alum saturating, drying again, and gently pressing on low heat. As with the silk scarves, with the two of us opposite each other holding the four corners, we center a scarf over the pattern, and lower the middle of it slowly. As the center touches down, we gradually allow the sides to follow, but slowly to prevent movement of the medium and (we hope) achieve smooth marbling throughout, free of air bubbles or white smears and streaks where no paint took hold.

White silk ties hand made in the Orient are available from some of the suppliers listed at the back of the book.

Italian Shell Pattern

*What can
go wrong
and what,
if anything,
to do about it.*

We have talked about the perils of no alum, or inadequate alum, but there are some other common problems that are avoidable.

It's important to keep all equipment, tools and supplies in the workplace clean and dry. The carrageenan powder should be stored in an airtight container in a cool, dry place, and only a clean, dry measuring spoon should dip into the powder. Without this precaution, mold may develop in the carrageenan powder. It's undetectable until the medium is prepared and you're ready to begin marbling; if there is mold, you'll notice a greasy-looking film on the medium's surface, or an unusual smell that is somewhat sour. The dead giveaway, though, is thin bands of brown that seem to float midway through the medium. When paints are dropped and you begin to manipulate the colors, the patterns break down rapidly, and what's

left on the surface begins to look like tiny paint chips rather than smooth, floating circles and veins of color. The only solution we know of is to throw away the medium and start over with new carrageenan and thoroughly cleaned equipment.

When there are air bubbles or little globs of paint on the medium amid your design, remove them before you lay down the prepared fabric. Air bubbles may burst when the cloth is placed on them and the result will be either a splashy break in pattern or just an area of no pattern. The little globs of paint will streak and run and look messy. You can pop the air bubbles with your fingertip or a straight pin, and the small globs

of paint can be either gently lifted off with the fingertip or a corner of a tissue, or pushed under with a stylus or pin. Removing small problems probably won't harm your design much, but if it does you can comb the surface again to make a new pattern before you lay down the prepared fabric.

Unfortunate streaks and smears can occur if the fabric is not laid down center first and allowed to drop gently and evenly in all directions. Pockets of air hold areas of the fabric away from the surface of the medium; if you try to push the fabric down with your fingertips, the trapped air moves the paint just enough to leave unpainted streaks on the piece. Streaks can also occur if the alum was unevenly applied, or if the fabric went through a dryer with a fabric softener sheet.

Dropping the fabric with a jerk will leave a blank line where the paint surface was disturbed. Loose threads on the surface of the medium will prevent the paint from taking there, leaving a white line on the fabric.

We use shadow marbling (see page 55) to correct pieces that were almost perfect but have small streaks, air bubbles, or a seam area that didn't print. We have salvaged many scarves this way. We recommend that you first experiment with the technique on 10-inch squares of cotton to see what can happen, then take a scarf or shirt that you're not satisfied with and re-alum, dry, and marble again. If the first pattern was intricately combed and contained several colors, you may want to shadow with only one color or the two main colors of the first marbling. But be careful—you can overdo it. I had a silk shawl first marbled in primary colors, swirled randomly. I then tried to add more green and white in simple circles, and after a third aluming I tried to add metallics. By that time, the shawl didn't look appealing enough to use for a cleanup cloth!

OTHER MEDIA

We tested many thickeners as marbling mediums before deciding to recommend carrageenan. There are a few articles in craft magazines about marbling with various substances, but for the most part we have found these other substances

We tested many other thickeners before deciding to recommend carrageenan.

unsatisfactory in both performance and price. We note costs of substances available in the Chicago area as of May 1989.

Carrageenan. One tablespoon of powder yields 1/2 gallon of medium. Seven to 8 gallons of medium will fill a 36-inch square frame, using 14 to 16 tablespoons of carrageenan. A pound of carrageenen costs about $20 by mail order, so the approximate cost for the large frame is $10. One and a half gallons of medium for a small container such as a roasting pan would cost $2. The large frame can be used for as long as ten to twelve days, and will hold up for as much as fifty yards of fabric. Simple to extremely complex patterns are achievable on the surface of carrageenan, and the medium is easy to clean up. It remains clear through repeated uses; you can see distinctly what paint is on the surface and how it is patterned, and what paint has fallen through or dropped to the bottom.

Sodium alginate. Like carrageenan, this is a seaweed derivative. It won't do as many yards as carrageenan and it is thicker and cloudier, but in many other respects it's a good second-place alternative. Good patterns can be achieved on its surface, it is ready to use in a short time, it is nontoxic, and it stores well. As far as we know, sodium alginate is available only by mail order. Currently it costs $12 per pound. It is mixed in approximately the same proportions as carrageenan so is only 60% of the cost. We have tried it only in small containers such as roasting pans. It never got as clear as carrageenan does, but stayed slightly thicker and golden in color. After an hour or two, it's hard to see what's on the bottom of the container or how much paint is exactly on the surface.

Liquid starch. This can be used directly from the bottle. It costs $2 per quart. You would need 6 quarts, or $12 worth, for a small container, 28 to 32 quarts, or $56 to $64 worth, for the 36-inch square frame. Fairly good patterns are achievable. However, some color intensity is lost immediately, as the starch carries some paint with it as it is rinsed. The surface of liquid starch medium can be skimmed clean of paint through several yards of fabric, but since the starch is opaque to begin with, it is harder to see how much of the paint is exactly on the surface ready to be picked up by the fabric.

Powdered starch. Argo powdered laundry starch is only $.85 per box, but we found it difficult to work with. Patterns of paint drifted off to the sides of the container, and the solution drying on our fingers was uncomfortable and itchy.

Egg white. Absolutely worthless, and besides, what would you do with all those yolks?

Wallpaper paste. A 4-ounce box of powder costs $4 at our local hardware store. A roasting pan (1 1/2 gallons of water) would take only about half the powder, or $2 worth. Simple random swirls are possible, though very intricate patterns are not. It is cloudy from the beginning, is not easily skimmed clean, and breaks down after a few uses. This substance, or perhaps the liquid starch, might do for an elementary school craft class or a Scout troop, but it's not a good alternative for an artist, or even a hobbyist who wants to marble T-shirts, scarves, or yards of fabric for special sewing.

Other techniques. After reading an article last Christmas on marbling glass ornaments, we tried a method (later demonstrated on the *Home Show* on ABC) that calls for spraying several colors of paint on the surface of a bucket of cold water, then lowering glass ornaments through the paints and slowly bringing them back up. The spray paints cost between $2 and $3 each; the box of six glass ornaments was $4. We tried nearly two dozen glass ornaments of various sizes and hues, and came up with only two that were uniformly marbled and usable. In most cases, the paint chipped off as soon as it dried or ran off while the ornaments hung to dry. Red and blue glass didn't take the paint at all.

We have also tried gelatin, fruit pectin, agar agar, and aloe vera as a marbling medium. These are easily obtainable substances, but they are not clear and they don't present a surface that can be manipulated into anything more than a random swirl. After they sit for a few hours, they all thicken and don't work at all. Aloe vera had its skin-softening property to recommend it, but we'd rather just use it as a lotion and forget trying to apply paint to it.

In pamphlets on marbling published by paint companies or art supply distributors, we've seen directions that simply start with pouring starch or the company's special secret, magical thickening agent (it's seaweed, but at $9 for 2 ounces it's also highway robbery: you can get the same seaweed for $20 per pound by mail order) into a roasting pan. Paints or dyes are then floated and manipulated, and unprepared fabric is placed on the medium. The fabric is not rinsed but is dried and then heat set. We have found that if we do not wash, dry and then prepare the fabric with alum, the colors will wash out every time. We've also consistently found that following pamphlet directions for marbling will give only the simplest swirling patterns, and these look grainy and uneven.

Peacock Pattern

*Sharing
the fun
with
children
and adults.*

If you are a teacher, recreation leader, or parent interested in teaching marbling to children, you can provide each child with a disposable aluminum roasting pan or cardboard box lined with plastic, some paints and mixing supplies, a stack of construction paper or cotton squares you've prepared in advance with alum, and some combs and toothpicks. Use liquid starch or wallpaper paste for the medium; the results aren't as good, but they are good enough for this simple use, and the materials are available at any grocery store or paint store.

If the group has been told in advance of the project, and they're all interested in marbling T-shirts, have embroidery hoops ready so they can print just one area, rinse well, and then take the dripping shirts home in plastic bags with dryer instructions for their parents.

Teaching marbling workshops to adults is fun, too. It's exciting to watch others as they first see a demonstration and moments later produce their own colorful and magical patterns. There's always a great deal of oohing and ahhing. Each workshop we've taught has reinforced our belief that anyone can learn this craft and in a few short hours come away with some fabric or paper that can be turned into something useful or pretty. People can go on to spend as much time as they want in their own kitchen or garage and, with a minimal investment in equipment and supplies, achieve an ever-increasing skill level in marbling.

Our workshops run from 10 A.M. until 3 P.M. and are typically offered on a Saturday or Sunday. We ask students to prepay so that receipt of their check is their registration. We currently charge $40 per student. After receiving their check, we send a confirmation letter which advises them of the date and time and that all supplies are covered by their fee. They're also advised to bring a sack lunch and to wear old clothes that they don't mind getting paint on. We provide coffee and tea.

The day before the workshop, we set up the marbling frame, fill it with medium, and thoroughly clean all other equipment and supplies, especially if they haven't been in use for a few weeks and have gathered dust. Then we take stock of our paints to make sure there's an adequate assortment. Next, we launder several yards of plain white fabric in cotton, cotton/ polyester blend, cotton/rayon twill, polyester, polyester satin, synthetic taffeta, and even some T-shirts. After they're dried, we alum everything and hang it. By morning, all the fabric is dry and ready to use. We then cut it into usable pieces.

Each student is given a roasting pan filled with medium and an assortment of prepared fabrics. Everyone is also given time to use the large 38-inch frame. We provide a handout that summarizes marbling techniques and lists suppliers and further reading suggestions. After talking about the process for about an hour, we demonstrate for another hour or so. We show all stages from preparing medium, to preparing fabric with alum, to mixing paints and adding oxgall, to dropping paint, creating patterns, laying fabric, rinsing, and hanging to dry. At this point, we usually take a short lunch break and then people start to work on their own. We circulate through the group, answering questions, offering advice and sharing their enthusiasm.

We always have prepared T-shirts and 1/2-pound quantities of carrageenan and alum for sale so that the most eager can go home and set up to marble right away. It's not only a fun day, but we find that we learn more about marbling each time we teach; usually someone has a question that hasn't come up before that sends us off on a new path of investigation.

Freestyle Pattern

Bouquet Pattern

alum: powdered form of aluminum sulfate crystals, used in marbling to assist the chemical bond of paint to fabric. A solution of water and alum is used to prepare fabric and paper to take on color permanently.

carrageenan: a fine powder extracted from dried seaweed found along the coast of Ireland; when mixed with water, it thickens the fluid and provides an ideal medium on which to float and manipulate paints, dyes, or inks for marbling (also known as carrageenin, carragheen, carragheenin, or Irish moss).

ebru: Turkish form of marbling on fine paper

medium: thickened water on which paints and dyes are floated and manipulated for marbling (also known as a size or marbling bath)

oxgall: a fluid found in the gallbladder of the ox, used by watercolorists and marblers to dilute paint by reducing the surface tension

resist: a product or process (such as ties, beeswax, or rice paste) which prevents dye or paint from being absorbed in a designated area of the fabric

shadow marbling: printing over a previously marbled paper or piece of fabric to produce a double-exposure effect (also known as overmarbling)

shenshi: a bamboo frame used in the Oriental form of marbling (*suminagashi*) on which fabric and paper are stretched taut

sizing: a temporary finish added to cloth by the manufacturer to give it its crisp, new look. Sizing must be washed out before marbling cloth.

sodium alginate: another seaweed derivative, it can be mixed with water and used in place of carrageenan as the marbling medium.

suminagashi: Japanese marbling; typically inks floating on plain water with little manipulation or interference, and with gentle movement encouraged by fanning or blowing on the paints. There are elements of philosophy and spirituality tied to this practice, and the patterns emerging look like natural phenomena.

BIBLIOGRAPHY

Ink and Gall, a quarterly journal for marblers published by Dexter Ing and edited by Polly Fox. Write to Box 1469, Taos, New Mexico 87571. A one-year subscription is $25 (foreign $30 by ship or $44 by air) and well worth it.

Fox, Polly, *Marbling on Fabric*. Fresh Ink Press, Box 1469, Taos, New Mexico 87571, 1990. $14.95 + $1.75 postage and handling.

The following books are available from Colophon Book Art Supply, 3046 Hogum Bay Road NE, Olympia, Washington 98507, (206) 459-2940; or from Basic Crafts/School Products, 1201 Broadway, New York, New York 10001, (800) 847-4127; in New York, (212) 679-3516:

Chambers, Anne, *The Practical Guide to Marbling Paper*. New York: Thames & Hudson, 1986.

Guyot, Don, *Suminagashi: An Introduction to Japanese Marbling*. Seattle Brass Galley Press, 1988.

Maurer, Paul, and Diane Philippoff Maurer, *An Introduction to Carrageenan and Watercolor Marbling*. Pennsylvania: self-published, 1984.

Nevins, Iris, *Traditional Marbling*. Sussex, New Jersey: self-published, 1985.

Nevins, Iris, *Fabric Marbling*. Sussex, New Jersey: self-published, 1989.

Basic Crafts, 1201 Broadway, New York, NY 10001, (800) 847-4127; in New York, (212) 679-3516. Bookbinding and marbling supplies, books. Catalog $3.

Brooks & Flynn, Inc., P. O. Box 2639, Rohnert Park, CA 94927-2639, (800) 822-2372 or (707) 584-7715. Paints, dyes, supplies, short instruction pamphlets. Call for a free catalog.

Cerulean Blue, P. O. Box 21168, Seattle, WA 98111-3168. Paints, dyes, sodium alginate, tools, fabrics. A wonderfully informative and colorful catalog for only $4.50.

Colophon Book Art Supply, 3046 Hogum Bay Road NE, Olympia, WA 98507, (206) 459-2940. Carrageenan, alum, colors, tools, books, video tapes.

Color Craft, 14 Airport Park Road, E. Granby, CT 06026, (800) 243-2712 or (203) 653-5505. Createx marbling colors, many other fabric dyes and paints as well as related tools and supplies.

Current, Inc. The Current Building, Colorado Springs, CO 80941. Envelopes and stationery supplies.

Decorative Papers, P. O. Box 749, Easthampton, MA 01027. Acrylic paints especially made for marbling from the formula developed by Iris Nevins, whose books are listed in the Bibliography.

Eisner Brothers, 760 Orchard Street, New York, NY 10002, (800) 426-7700 or (212) 475-6868, Sunday through Thursday. T-shirts galore, every size and style imaginable with the lowest prices if you are ordering by the dozens.

Ruppert, Gibbon, and Spider, 718 College Street, Healdsburg, CA 95448, (707) 433-9577. Silk samples $17. They sell scarves, ties, silks and cottons, brushes and tools, and a full line of Jacquard and Deka paints and dyes.

Sureway Trading Enterprises, 826 Pine Avenue, Suites 5 and 6, Niagara Falls, NY, (416) 596-1887. Silks, cottons, linens.

Talas, 218 W. 35th Street, New York, NY 10001-1996, (212) 736-7744. Marbling supplies, dyes and paints, books.

Test Fabrics, P. O. Box 420, 200 Blackford Avenue, Middlesex, NJ 08846, (201) 469-6446. Fabrics of all kinds at competitive prices.

Thai Silks, 252 State Street, Los Altos, CA 94022, (800) 722-SILK or (415) 948-8611. Large variety of silks, silk blends, and other fabrics, some finished garments, and an excellent selection of inexpensive, hand-hemmed silk scarves in many sizes. Also ready-made white silk ties.

CHECKLIST OF EQUIPMENT & SUPPLIES

For the marbling frame:

- shallow, light-colored pan OR four pieces of 1-inch by 4-inch wood, two of the length and two of the width of the desired frame size
- four flat metal angles and sixteen screws to go with them
- screwdriver and carpenter's angle
- shower curtain, drop cloth, or other clear or light-colored plastic sheeting
- eight push pins or thumbtacks

For mixing the medium:

- carrageenan
- distilled water
- bucket
- blender (for blender carrageenan)

- stove, metal pan, and stick or wooden spoon (for heated carrageenan)

For preparing the fabric:

- alum (aluminum sulfate)
- tap water
- nonmetal bucket or pan

For mixing paints:

- acrylic paints or airbrush dyes
- oxgall
- stirring tools such as popsicle sticks or plastic spoons
- small containers for mixing and storing

For applying paints:

- chopsticks, toothpicks, or other sticks

- broomstick whisk
- eyedropper

For creating patterns:

- combs
- marbling rake
- toothpicks or other stylus

Fabrics, and papers:

- smooth, textured papers or pieces of cloth, cut to the size of the marbling frame and prepared in the alum bath

Drying and setting:

- clothesline with pinch-type pins
- household iron

I N D E X

acrylic paints   15, 18–19, 25, 78
agar agar medium   83
air bubbles   22–23, 27, 74, 79, 81
airbrush paints   19
aloe vera medium   83
alum   15, 24, 61, 81, 83
aluminum sulfate   15
appliqué   68–71

bibliography   90
blender carrageenan   18, 21, 23
blouse, marbled   70, 77
book bag, marbled   74
bookmarks   67
bouquet pattern   28, 88, 48–49

care of marbled fabrics   30
carrageenan   15, 18, 21, 82
cascade pattern   40–41, 57–58
Chinese marbling   13
clothing   13, 60–63, 68–71, 72–74, 77–79
color mixing   25, 31
combed pattern   38–39
combing the pattern   27, 32–33
consistency of paint   25, 57

disposal of medium   29–30
distilled water   18
drip bucket   16
dropping paint   27, 32–33
drying fabric   16, 24, 29, 32–33

ebru   13
egg white medium   15–16, 83
embroidery hoop   61–62
equipment and supplies   16–17, 20, 92
European marbling   13

fabric choice   19, 57, 69, 77–78
fabric dyes   18–19, 20
fabric preparation   24, 60, 77–78
feather pattern   44–45, 57–58
formaldehyde   29
freestyle pattern   36–37
fruit pectin medium   83

gelatin medium   83
glossary   89

heated carrageenan   18, 21, 22

Irish moss   15

jacket   69, 71
Japanese marbling   13

kimono project   76–78

laying fabric on medium   28, 32–33
liquid starch medium   15–16, 82, 85

mail order   15, 91
marble bag   59
marbling bath   15
marbling comb   20, 39
marbling frame   17, 18, 78
marbling process   27–30, 32–33
medium   15–17, 82–83
modular clothing   70
mold in carrageenan   29, 81

neckties, marbled   78–79
nonpareil pattern   42–43
note card project   64–67

oil paint   13
ornaments, marbled   65–66, 83
other marbling media   82–83
overmarbling   54–55
oxgall   15, 19, 25

paint application   27
paint globs   25, 29, 81
paint preparation   25
Palowoda, Marie   75
paper marbling   64–67
patterns   27–28, 32–33, 34–55
Persian marbling   13
pieced jacket project   68–71
pillow project   56–59
plastic-covered cardboard   16, 29, 58
powdered starch medium   82–83

quilting   68–71

rainbow stripes   59
rinsing fabric   28–29, 32–33, 58

scarves, marbled   78–79
seaweed   15, 83
setting color   29, 32–33, 58, 62
shadow marbling   54–55, 74, 77, 82
Shaker boxes, marbled   75
Sir Francis Bacon   13
size   15
sizing   24
skimming   15, 16, 21–23, 27, 29, 32–33, 58
skirt, marbled   70
sodium alginate medium   82
sources and suppliers   91
Spanish marbling   12, 13
starch medium   82–83
stone pattern   34–35, 57
storing carrageenan   29
streaks   24, 78–79, 81
suminagashi   13
supplies   18–19
surface tension   15, 25

teaching   11, 85–86
temperature of air   11, 17
tennis shoe project   72–74
testing paint   25
three-dimensional objects, marbled   62, 72–75, 78
tips and techniques   81–83
tools   20–21, 27
Turkish marbling   13
T-shirt plastic insert   62, 77
T-shirt project   60–63, 85

wallpaper paste medium   15–16, 83, 85
washing marbled fabrics   30, 32–33, 58, 62
water   15, 18, 22–23
wave pattern   52–53, 57–58
whisk, broomstick   20, 27, 47
white line on fabric   82
wings pattern   50–51
wood, marbled   65–66, 75
work space   16
workshops   85

zebra pattern   46–47